EXPLORING THE NEW FAMILY

Kathleen O'Connell Chesto, DMin

Parents and their
young adults in transition

EXPLORING
THE NEW
FAMILY

Saint Mary's Press   Christian Brothers Publications   Winona, Minnesota

Genuine recycled paper with 10% post-consumer waste.
Printed with soy-based ink.

The publishing team included Robert P. Stamschror, consulting editor; Leif Kehrwald, development editor; Rebecca Fairbank, copy editor; Barbara Bartelson, production editor; Hollace Storkel, typesetter; Cären Yang, cover designer; manufactured by the production services department of Saint Mary's Press.

Printed in the United States of America

Printing: 9 8 7 6 5 4 3 2 1

Year: 2009 08 07 06 05 04 03 02 01

ISBN 0-88489-599-8

Library of Congress Cataloging-in-Publication Data

Chesto, Kathleen O.
    Exploring the new family : parents and their young adults in transition / Kathleen O'Connell Chesto.
        p. cm.
Includes bibliographical references.
        ISBN 0-88489-599-8 (pbk.)
        1. Young adults—United States—Interviews. 2. Young adults—Canada—Interviews. 3. Young adults—United States—Family relationships. 4. Young adults—Canada—Family relationships. 1. Title.
        HQ799.7 .C44 2001
        305.235'0973—dc21
                                        2001000753

To Jon, Becky, and Liz
who taught us how to be parents,
and to all the other wonderful young adults
they have brought into the life of our family.

This book could not have been written without the help of many persons. Sincere thanks to my son, Jon, for much of the initial research and interviewing as well as his writing and final editing. Thanks to my daughters, Becky and Liz, whose insights are also found here and who, with Jon, have shaped my own attitudes toward this stage of family life. Thanks to Steve and to Josh, the young men who came into my daughters' lives and offered another dimension to my understanding. To my husband, who has taught me so much about parenting and whose patience and support allow me to write, goes a huge debt of gratitude.

Thanks to the families who filled out the initial questionnaires, to those who consented to telephone interviews, and to those parents and young adults who willingly shared stories at my workshops around the country. Thanks to Valerie Oakley, research librarian at the Southbury Public Library, whose assistance with the initial research and final documentation was invaluable and saved many long hours. And thanks finally to the editor, Bob Stamschror of Saint Mary's Press, who waited so patiently for this book to be completed.

CONTENTS

ARE WE THERE YET?

The cookies are long gone,
the last of the juice drained from the sippy cups,
the songs on the children's cassette,
upbeat and funny an hour ago,
have become annoying,
to you and to us.
As we point out one more cow
toddler voices from the backseat
become a whine:
"Are we there yet?"
Not yet.

The license plate game has turned stale,
and you've grown too old for the cows.
The few songs we can harmonize
have worn themselves out.
The snacks were finished
ten minutes after we left.
A fight has broken out in the backseat:
"He crossed my line," "She's in my space."
We've drawn the imaginary lines,
and the temporary quiet is
broken by the hesitant question,
"Are we there yet?"
Not yet.

The radio is blaring
as we argue over stations
and volume control.
Feet stretch out around our heads
and through our windows.
The backseat is littered with cassettes
and the detritus of diet sodas,
cookies, and chips,
as the voice of boredom speaks:
"Are we there yet?"
Not yet.

The car is weighted down,
with bike and stereo, clothes and books,
old furniture and new towels,
pillows and posters,
mismatched dishes and pots and pans.
The memories of years
carefully packed in laundry baskets
fill the seat behind us.
The snacks sit untouched between us,
and a sacred quiet has fallen.
You break the silence first.
Apprehension, pride, excitement
all echo in your question,
"Are we there yet?"
Almost.

INTRODUCTION

GRADUATION 1993 BY JON CHESTO

NOTHING remains more vivid about graduation day than my intense feeling of disorientation as I raced around the grassy college quad at Wesleyan University seeking good-byes in the form of hugs, phone numbers, and addresses, desperately trying to hold on to a few pieces of the life that was leaving us behind.

I scanned the red-robed crowds across Andrus Field, searching for friends whom I would likely never see again. The throngs rapidly dissipated into anonymous station wagons and minivans filled with futons, milk crates, and other trappings of college life. Almost all that was left on that windswept lawn were rows of empty white chairs, many of them knocked over or pushed to the side, and the occasional discarded gown or commencement program.

The scene resembled the aftermath of a battle that had abruptly ended and the soldiers had just walked away. The war is over. Send the troops back home.

But where is home? Like soldiers returning from the front, our old world hadn't changed as much as we had during the time we were gone. Old rules and familiar faces didn't provide the comfort and structure they once did. Instead, they felt more like the bars of a prison meant to keep us safe from ourselves.

The thousands of us whose highways took us away from our colleges and universities on those sunny, early summer days of 1993 were faced with a dizzying choice of avenues, dark alleys, and grand boulevards without a road map in sight.

For as long as we could remember, the next step in our lives had been charted ahead of time. Grade after grade rolled by at an increasingly quick pace. By the time we were seniors, we were being told which colleges we should apply to and how to go about filling in the requisite forms to get us there.

Collegiate life offered us many simple freedoms in the new decisions we had to make. Which laundry detergent should we buy? Does it make more sense to buy a quart of milk or a gallon? Where's the best place in town to get a car fixed? obtain a new bank account? get a haircut? But the path was still laid out, plain and clear: four more years of school, broken up by the familiar rhythms of summer vacations, weeks off at Christmastime, and a long weekend at Thanksgiving.

The thousands of us whose highways took us away from our colleges and universities on those sunny, early summer days of 1993 were faced with a dizzying choice of avenues, dark alleys, and grand boulevards without a road map in sight.

As the end of senior year approached, we felt something big was about to happen, but we didn't know exactly what. Apprehension bound us together in more ways than we realized. We spent nights agonizing over a paper on the Christian missionary movements of the New World, or the influence of Elizabethan society on Shakespeare's plays, but the real stresses came from the fact that we could never read enough to learn in which direction our future would take us. After traversing the sidewalks of familiar downtown streets for most of our lives, the sidewalks had run out. The roads before us led away from the well-lit life of our childhood through the unfamiliar darkness on the edge of town.

I was relatively lucky. I worked as a newspaper reporter after graduation, and soon decided, despite long hours and low pay, that this was the career for me. Newspaper wages being what they are, I stayed with my parents for a year before saving enough money to live on my own. Eventually I was sharing an apartment with friends, worrying about heating bills and car repairs, and working long hours at a job I enjoyed, certifying me as an adult in a grown-up world.

Other classmates were not as fortunate. Some moved to cities on the other side of the continent, following a lover or a dream, only to feel disconnected by the separation from the past they left behind. Some took on high-paying jobs in Manhattan, settling for the money and the job, never realizing their dreams of becoming a film director or novelist.

Most of us had developed a solid self-image by that point, but a critical link was missing: How did we fit in with the rapidly changing society around us?

The struggle to complete our identity by resolving how we connected with others manifested itself in many ways. Our relationships with our family had shifted. Now there was an expectation that we start our own family yet still keep our roles in the family that had nurtured us.

We no longer found and kept friends in convenient places such as the classroom, the locker room, the dorm hall, or the bus stop. Few of us carved out time to really get to know the strange new places where we lived, let alone to vote in municipal elections. The structure of organized religion seemed anachronistic, although many of us felt the loss of the foundation provided by rituals like church or synagogue services.

Through it all, we struggled to find ways to fund our freedom. College bills, rent checks, and car loans limited where we could live and what we could do once we got there.

Seven more classes have received their college diplomas since I walked away from Andrus Field. Some have settled down with houses, spouses, and careers. Others have yet to discover a place where the ground is as solid as Wesleyan's well-manicured lawns.

Looking back, many of us tried to fool ourselves into thinking the search for our adult identity had been accomplished by the time we graduated from college.

But I think we knew better. I think we knew it had just begun.

ABOUT THIS BOOK BY KATHLEEN CHESTO

Some books are carefully constructed, design following the scaffolding that supports the building process. Some books begin with a germ of an idea and grow into something even the author did not expect. This book began as the former and ended as the latter. Originally meant to be a manual on the "launching stage" of family life, designed to offer support in navigating the young adult's transition to independence while fostering adult friendship in families, it slowly took on a life of its own.

Back when I was still building a scaffolding around the necessary steps toward growing an adult family, it became obvious that my own experience as parent represented only half of the picture. I sought the collaboration of my adult son to give the book a more balanced approach, a respect for the needs and viewpoints of all involved in the issues, a book for both parents and young adults. Because the experience of our family has been fairly limited—all three young adults followed the same pattern of leaving home for college, graduating in four years, then taking a year to become established before moving out—we sought input from other families across the United States and Canada, interviewing those whose lives reflected more varied experiences.

The scaffolding began to crumble as Jon and I argued over the issues, over their significance, over the differing views of the two generations. The book that evolved became very like our discussion, an attempt to develop insight and understanding into the different family that is emerging in our own home as well as homes across our country. The issues and challenges that face young people today, how they differ from those that existed a generation ago, and how parents are seeking to help young adults grow up and grow out, became the primary focus. We discovered we had no answers, and so we centered on the questions. We focused on attempting to provide the framework that would help other families to communicate, eventually finding their own answers.

In exploring the issues, we relied on three types of experts: the other authors in the field, the communal wisdom of the dedicated parents across the United States and Canada, and the insights of the visionary, hopeful young adults who have been willing to share their thoughts with us. The text was shaped and focused by their responses.

Halfway through the germination process, my son's career took him out of state (more crumbling scaffolding). Although the book still strongly reflects his research and interviewing skills, it became necessary for me to write the text from my own viewpoint as parent. The limits imposed by distance and the demands of a new job simply made the dual voice approach we had hoped to use too difficult to maintain. When I felt the need for more of the young adult voice than my son could provide, I turned to my daughters and accepted their insights, journal pieces, and poetry as contrast. The resulting book may not demonstrate the balance Jon and I had originally tried to achieve, but it accurately reflects the ordinary changes and ever-present upheavals of family life that it was designed to address.

This is not a book about "how" but a book about "who."

This is not a book about "how" but a book about "who." It is not a theoretical reflection on how we foster maturity as much as it is a long look at the young adults who are emerging in our families and the influences, within us and beyond us, that have shaped them. Because it is more flesh than theory, it became difficult at times to look at the young adult *stage* of family life without reflecting specifically on the particular generation presently living it.

I would like to believe this is not a book strictly for parents, even though it is written by a parent. It is the hope of my son and myself that this book will belong to all of us who are willing to work at discovering better ways to support each other in the process of becoming whole individuals and healthy adult families.

Nihil est ab omni parte beatum.

"Nothing is an unmixed blessing."

—**HORACE**

Chapter 1

TALKING SENSE

PARENTING is a terminal illness. It begins with the conception of the first child and lasts until death. We may send them off to nursery school, to camp, to college and careers, to spouses and homes of their own, but we never stop being their parents. We worry as much about the first day on a new job as we worried about the first day of kindergarten. No matter how psychologically astute we may be, no matter how much we recognize that we rear them in order to let them go, with each of their successes comes a secret sense of satisfaction, with each of their failures the nagging question, "Where did we go wrong?" This parental illness is not something we admit readily, not to our friends, to our spouses, or even to ourselves. But it surfaces unbidden during the sleepless nights that can still haunt us long after childhood fevers have been replaced by broken relationships and damaged dreams. In our most excruciatingly honest moments, we admit that there is no escape. This is a book for all of us who share this condition, and for those who are the source of our concerns.

The years following high school graduation to the midtwenties hold the most serious of all developmental tasks for families. We parents are attempting to move on to a life no longer focused around children, while helping our

The years following high school graduation to the midtwenties hold the most serious of all developmental tasks for families.

young adults become established in their own lives. We anguish over when it is best to offer insights from experience and when it is best to let young adults learn from their own failures. When does advice become interference? When does a little financial support become financial dependence? When does a safety net become a snare?

At the same time, our young adults are attempting to complete the separation begun in adolescence while healing some of the alienation that period may have created. It is hoped that they are beginning to develop intimate peer relationships with the capability of creating their own families while also establishing themselves in a career or job that gives them financial independence. As parents we work at remaining connected to them even as we are accepting separation and independence. Our successful navigation of this transition may mean developing respect for careers and occupations far removed from our own cherished dreams, and for lifestyles and emotional attachments we would not have chosen. The goal of the family is for young adults to succeed in developing their own views and separate identities without emotionally cutting themselves off from their parents.

Negotiating this period of family life has become increasingly difficult in our society simply because that society is changing so rapidly. The parents of today's young adults are products of a generation in which we were expected to finish high school and get on with our lives. Some of us went to college; the vast majority of us left home and did not return for more than a visit. Anything else was considered "failure." The choices offered to most of us were limited by our family resources, the environment in

Extending the years of education has extended the years of dependency.

which we grew up, and our sex. Today much more is available, and we want more for our children; we offer a plethora of possibilities and then become frustrated by their inability to decide.

The complex nature of today's career choices has made a bachelor's degree as crucial to the attainment of the "good life" as a high school diploma once was, and extending the years of education has extended the years of dependency. The availability of college financing, loans, and grants, and the greater visibility of college programs, have offered the possibility of a college education to an increasing number of young adults,[1] further inflating the number of youth delaying independence. This availability of financing coupled with the escalating cost of college have resulted in a generation beginning its adult life more deeply in debt than any other group in history.

This indebtedness helps to explain, at least in part, young adults' surprising willingness to remain at home. Independent living is a difficult, if not impossible, choice for many. However, the decision to remain at home deprives both parents and young adults of the distance that once enabled youth to become independent and helped their parents to view them as having identities separate from their family of origin.

The task of achieving maturity has been further complicated by the media and computer technology that have foisted a psychosocial and sexual maturity on increasingly younger children. Health and nutrition standards are creating an earlier physical maturity, at the same time that economic independence has moved later. This dissonance in the lives of our young adults is reflected in the stress placed on the developmental stage known as the launching family,[2] the period of time in which adolescents become established as independent adults while their parents move on to a life not centered on child rearing.

Current popular sociology argues that this combination of social and cultural developments has led to a delay in the launching period and an extension of adolescence to the age of thirty.[3] The young adults and parents we interviewed do not agree with this assessment. If you consider the characteristics common to the teen years, it becomes obvious that today's young adults are not adolescents, "extended" or otherwise. Adolescents tend to view themselves as entitled to whatever their parents provide. Young adults returning home today are more likely to see themselves as the recipients of their parents' hospitality. Concepts of money have become tinged with a realism that carries a concomitant respect for parents as fellow laborers in the workforce. Peer groups, so crucial to adolescent identity, are losing their influence as the twenty-somethings move from separating from family to attempts to reintegrate with family.

Today's rapidly changing culture is producing a new stage of psychosocial development. I have chosen to call this stage "postadolescence."

It is true that many of these young people are not quite "launched." They are not quite independent adults, but they are not adolescents. This is an age that straddles adolescence and adulthood. Just as in recent history mandatory education created the stage of development we now call adolescence, today's rapidly changing culture is producing a new stage of psychosocial development. I have chosen to call this stage postadolescence.[4]

Postadolescence, even though it is yet to be recognized as a true developmental stage, already runs the risk of becoming labeled with the same horror stories that have riddled adolescence for years. Today the very term *adolescent* is enough to make the mother of a preschooler cringe. Before pejorative terms like the "postponed" or "boomerang" generation have become as permanently ingrained in our mind-set as "rebellious teen" and "terrible two's," we have the opportunity to create a more positive myth capable of assisting us in this new period of transition from adolescent separation to adult friendship.

In attempting to articulate a myth for this new adult family, we begin with the assumption that all of us are affected by the culture in which we live, regardless of our personal circumstances. The unusual child who comes home from school to a stay-at-home mom and milk and cookies is still part of a latchkey generation and is influenced by the pressures and realities created by this phenomenon. The young adult who may be one of a family of seven with parents who are celebrating their thirtieth wedding anniversary is still part of a community shaped by divorce, unmarried parents, and smaller families. Although the cultural influences described in this book may not be the experiences of the individual, the world in which each of us lives has still been shaped by those influences.

Many of the issues discussed here are undoubtedly oversimplified. This book is not meant to provide answers, to lay blame, to delineate definitive causes. It lacks the scientific accuracy of a controlled sociological study. It is simply meant to present the possibility of a new phase of adult development and to open a discussion of its issues.

Many of the insights of the book are limited somewhat by an unintentional middle-class, higher education emphasis. True, this was our family experience. More important, it was also the experience of 165 of the 167 people who answered our original questionnaire or consented to be interviewed.

In attempting to expand this base, we discovered that postadolescence itself may have a middle-class bias. Unlike the extended education that created adolescence, the extended education that has done so much to lengthen the period of launching is not mandatory. Therefore, the phenomenon has not yet touched every family in our society. But the 67 percent of young adults seeking education beyond high school have become the norm, and as such their experience dominated our research. We also discovered "launching" to be more of an issue in families where young adults had grown accustomed to economic security and where parents had the luxury of thinking reflectively about the process.

If there is an intentional bias in the book, it is in favor of the young adults and of recognizing their contributions. These new postadolescents are not sleeping away these "interim" years, fingers permanently pressed on the alarm clock's snooze button. They are volunteering in larger numbers than ever before. They are swelling the ranks of professional doctors, lawyers, and engineers with an influx of both sexes. And they are generally exhibiting greater trust in their parents, confiding in them to an extent the previous generation would never have considered. As such this new generation of young adults embodies not only a new stage in social development but a profound cultural shift.

This book invites parents and young adults to begin the discussion on what has brought us to this point, how we can make it work, and what shape the new family will have. Any insights this book offers

If there is an intentional bias in the book, it is in favor of the young adults and recognizing their contributions.

are from the young adults and parents themselves and reflect a hopefulness that this stage, while holding its own specific problems and crises, also holds the potential of a new friendship that may yet prove to be one of the deepest satisfactions of parenthood and postadolescence.

I am a jack-o-lantern.
Somebody has cut me open and stolen my stem.
Somebody has taken a spoon and dug out my insides,
and thrown them on some newspaper to be taken out
to the trash.
Somebody has carved me a face
with a crooked smile and sparkling eyes.
They stuck a candle inside of me,
and now I light their way in the dark,
now I am their homecoming.
But candles don't burn forever,
and what's my use when the wick is burned
and the candle is melted?

—LIZ, AGE EIGHTEEN

Chapter 2

A SENSE
OF SELF

A MOTHER of three young adults in the northern Midwest re-counted the following story about her eldest son.

He was in his twenties, living in his own apartment, and working full-time at a Home Depot. He was a part-time student at the state university, between girlfriends, exercising, and watching his weight. And he was becoming extremely depressed. He approached his Mom in desperation.

"I have to quit work and go back to school full-time and get finished so I can start living my life!"

His bewildered mother said, "This *is* your life. You are living it."

"No, Mom, my *real* life," was the discouraged response.

We live in a world where we are defined by what we do. Go to any cocktail party. The first question anyone asks is, "What is your name?" The second, invariably, is, "What do you do?" And once we have answered that question, we can watch the inquirer summing us up, deciding how well educated we are, how intelligent we are, and perhaps, how wealthy we are. The entire scrutiny is designed to *identify* us, to help the other to decide if we are worth his or her time and conversation.

Anyone who has chosen to stay at home to raise a family knows the discomfort of those moments. Anyone who has chosen a "blue-collar" occupation or a profession simply seen as lower profile on an imaginary scale of importance knows the sense of being discounted and belittled as the interrogator tries to escape gracefully. We try to convince ourselves that we live in a classless society where all are equal. Anyone who has spent time at business parties, country clubs, and such knows that some are more equal than others. The difference between our class society and that of India is that we are not born into an ironclad caste. We ultimately choose our class by what we do with our lives. That is not to say that the choice is not severely limited or greatly enhanced by what we were born into, it is simply to say that true identity does not rest with our family or our hometown, if we even had one.

We have become a people known by what we do.

It was not always this way. We were once a people of place, a people known by the town where our forebears came from, the town in which we probably grew up. Acclaimed sociologist Emile Durkheim warned at the beginning of the twentieth century that modern humanity was losing this sense of place,[1] a warning largely overlooked in his day, that has become prophetic in our own. We have become a people known by what we do.

This form of identity has inherent problems. The first has become obvious as the nation ages. If you are what you do, who are you when you are no longer able to do it? Despite the growth of retirement villages and advertising aimed at an older leisure class, as well as a new vision of retirement as a time of opportunity, the truth we have created about the relationship between identity and work remains deeply ingrained in our subconscious. When Charles Schulz died on the day the last *Peanuts* strip appeared in our papers, news commentators spoke of "how fitting" that it should happen this way. The life of this sensitive man who graced our century with such gentle, humorous insight into childhood and reflected adulthood was viewed as complete once he stopped working for the rest of us. In a rural

Connecticut town, when one of the last family farms was sold to make room for a new high school, the farmer, a man of fifty-one years, died the day his produce stand closed. Again people said "how fitting." The implication is that the central, perhaps the only, value of our lives is in the work we do. It raises the question our youngest child raised in her poem on the jack-o-lantern, the poem that began this discussion: Who are we after the candle has burned and your use for us has ended?

The flip side of the problem is becoming more obvious as our children take longer to mature. If you are what you do, then who are you *before* you are ready to do it? If you are "one of the O'Connells from Cork," as my own father was, you are that from the moment you are born. If you are your work, your profession, your career, you may well spend a lifetime attempting to discover who you are.

Consequently, we live in an age where we search for our identity, a concept our own grandparents would find ludicrous. My grandfather frequently comforted me as a child when my efforts fell short by saying, in his thick Irish brogue, "You be what you be, me girl." Not anymore, Grandad, not anymore. "What do you want to be when you grow up?" has taken on the sinister implication that you are not really anything yet.

We who parent today's twenty-year-olds represent the transition from centuries of belonging to land and family, from "being who you be" to the disintegration of an identity determined by family and place. We have made ourselves responsible for our own identity. It is a self-determination principle of which this country is incredibly proud, but which, in reality, adds another dimension to the already difficult task of growing up. What we correctly perceive as freedom also

What we correctly perceive as freedom also involves a loss of a sense of self and its accompanying sense of security.

involves a loss of a sense of self and its accompanying sense of security.

Add to that loss a bewildering array of possibilities, and it is no wonder that our children are taking longer to "grow up," or, in the classic jargon, "find themselves." When I was a child, I may not have known who I was as surely as my father had known at my age, but what I was going to become was fairly well determined. I was a girl; I was good in school; therefore, I would be a teacher or a nurse. Or I could become a nun who would be a teacher or a nurse. Certainly some women my age became doctors and lawyers and electricians and pilots, but I did not know any of them and it never appeared as a choice to me. Theater, my own secret passion, would have been only slightly more acceptable to my immigrant parents than prostitution.

My choices may have been limited, but they were part of an integrated whole, a small portion of what my life would be. There was a sense that my future, my sense of self, would be far more determined by the family I myself chose to create than by anything I chose to do. The choice to teach was a source of livelihood, not identity. "Something to fall back on when the children are grown" is what my own mother called it.

And so we have a new generation that takes longer making the choices, not necessarily because of some intrinsic failure on our part or theirs, but perhaps simply because they have been offered so many choices, and the options have become so significant. They struggle with "job satisfaction" straight out of high school. If your work is who you are, all the more reason to need to like it. It is no longer simply the necessary piece by which we once funded our real lives. It is their real life.

As careers require an increasing amount of education and training, the number of young people seeking college degrees has increased steadily while the worth of a high school diploma has devalued just as swiftly. Choosing college, for those who take that route, is frequently becoming a monumental project, involving all the years of high school. After all, it is shaping what they do and therefore who they are. It is a limiting choice in a world that has, up to this point, offered only ever-expanding ones. Too often their leisure as well as their study, the sports they play and the activities they join, fall under the guiding influence of the expectations of the colleges they hope to attend.

Once in college they change majors frequently or leave them undeclared as long as possible. And each change involves a subsequent loss of identity because they no longer want to *do* what they thought they did. They struggle to complete four-year programs in five years as they move from one field to another. Once back home it may take another few years before they figure out their "real lives."

For the young adults who choose not to go to college, job becomes an even larger source of identity. The parents of this group spoke consistently about wanting their children to find something they loved, something that "turned them on" as a way to establish themselves as adults. The young adults echoed the sentiments of their parents, but society's focus on higher education has also made their search more difficult.

Today's high schools offer increasingly more college preparation courses and fewer and fewer vocational occupational training courses. The "commercial course" in high school that once attracted half of the average high school population and led to immediate entrance into the job market is a thing of the past. Auto shop, mechanics, and carpentry no longer have a place in our "college-charged" high schools, and so our young people are graduating with fewer skills. The administrative and secretarial jobs that commercial course students once sought now fall into that group of skills requiring advanced education degrees, an associate's degree if not a bachelor's. The lack of decent wages at the remaining entry-level positions, plus the lack of public transportation to get to the jobs, share responsibility with our limited secondary education for the delayed maturity of our non-college youth. The fact that these are not personal but large social issues over which families have little control makes the postadolescent period equally, if not more, challenging for this group of young adults.

For those of us who parent today's generation of postadolescents, it can be difficult for us to remember how much easier it was to "find ourselves" before life became so complicated.

For those of us who parent today's generation of postadolescents, it can be difficult for us to remember how much easier it was to "find ourselves" before life became so complicated. As the products of a far more limited world, we have often thought how fortunate, how incredibly blessed our own children are to have so many worlds of opportunity open to them. Many of us have struggled to give them the chances we wish had been ours, so it is understandable if we view their "opportunity" through rose-colored glasses. It is easy to forget that the choices have become more gut-wrenching, holding an importance that makes them frightening in their magnitude and bewildering in their expansiveness.

When our youngest child graduated from an excellent college and passed the entrance exam for medical school, we thought she had the world on a string. Her own perspective, given in the poem on the next page, threw a different light on that world of opportunity.

TIRED FEET

The canvas is blank and they ask me to paint
pick a brush, your palette is clean, here are some colors
mix and match, create your own,
think of the fun, the possibility . . . the freedom
the canvas is BLANK?!
shit, what will I draw?

feet tired, compass broke—walking on.

the stage is empty and they ask me to build
all the wood you need—oak is strong, pine fresh,
new tools, screws and nails galore
there might even be blueprints
think of the fun, the possibility . . . the freedom
the stage is EMPTY?!
shit, how do I create?

feet tired, compass broke—walking on.

The tide is going out and they ask me to catch it
the thunder has found its voice and they ask me to calm it
the sky has chosen dawn and they ask me to find the stars

the page has no words and they ask for inspiration
windows 95, a crappy printer and spell check
tell the stories, remember the memories, name the future
think of the fun, the possibility . . . the freedom
the page has NO words?!
shit! where do I begin?
do I even speak this language?

feet tired, compass broke . . . moving on.

— LIZ, AGE TWENTY-ONE

If we are what we do, the geometric progression of complexity in today's working world will make it increasingly more difficult for each successive generation to "find themselves." The rapidity with which the changes are occurring means that many of our young people are preparing for jobs that do not yet exist. In an article on the twenty-one hot-track careers for the twenty-first century, *U.S. News and World Report* listed, among others: "broadband architect, intensivist, technology recycler, tissue engineer."[2] My spell checker does not even recognize them. Identity, struggling to adapt, for our young adults, is becoming increasingly more dependent on employability and less dependent on specific employment.[3]

Relationship also fails to offer the secure identity it tried to promise to the parents of today's young adults. Ours was a generation that feared intimacy and sought commitment, our reasons colored as much by security as they were by morality. Our children's generation fears commitment and hungers for intimacy. Both the frequency and the ease of divorce has undermined the notion that a sense of self can be defined in and through commitment. Today's young adults want to "find themselves" first, trying on how a particular relationship fits before they make a commitment. This may be the faithful choice in a world where sexual promiscuity is promoted, and prenuptial agreements are often signed before a public vow of "forever" is made. "I can't be right for somebody else if I'm not right for me."[4] The song belonged to our generation. The sentiment belongs to theirs.

Relationship also fails to offer the secure identity it tried to promise to the parents of today's young adults.

Commitment for our generation has failed to support the burden of identity that we placed on it. For those of us who have maintained a committed relationship, the definition of identity has become of far less significance in our relationship than mutual support for one another's search.

We have left behind the time when we defined ourselves by the land that nurtured us. We are quickly moving to a time in which it is becoming increasingly difficult to define ourselves by what we do or by the primary relationships within which we choose to live. It may be time to stop defining ourselves by what is outside of us and begin looking inside, time to return to the ancient concept of vocation, to the idea that all of us are called and gifted. When identity is no longer anchored in a particular career, it has the possibility of becoming the sum total of the skills, talents, and experiences that make many varied careers possible. When identity is no longer based on relationship, it can be the sum total of the relational strengths and faithful attitudes that make committed relationships possible. Preparation for life in this situation is based not on what we hope to do or the family we hope to have but on the development of the potential we have been given.

We were all made for happiness. To understand what gives us happiness, to know what allows us to feel fulfilled and peaceful, and to be willing to choose to do that will be giant steps toward understanding who we are. Finding someone not to "make us happy" but to share the happiness we work at creating will enhance that fulfillment and understanding.

We are presently evolving in our understanding of the mysteries of the world around us. We hope that what we are witnessing in our young is also an evolution in our understanding of the world within us. God did not make us simply for work or only for one another. God made us to know, love, and serve, in and through one another, and to be happy, both in this life and the next.

Home is the place where, when you have to
go there, they have to take you in.

— ROBERT FROST, "THE DEATH OF THE HIRED MAN"[1]

Chapter 3

A SENSE
OF PLACE

THE INTRODUCTION to the conference had been long and rather routine. The host listed all the college degrees and awards of the speaker, as well as the published books and articles. The thousand or so parents listened politely, making the rustling sounds common to a distracted and inattentive audience. The host finished by informing the audience that the speaker lived with her husband and "any adult children who happened to be home at that time." A moment of absolute silence was quickly followed by a ripple of laughter, rueful grins, and nods of recognition. The connection was instantaneous and powerful. Despite the variety of ages of the parents present, the "home again" youth were a phenomenon with which the majority of the audience was well acquainted.

They have been called the revolving door generation. The U.S. Census Bureau reported an 85 percent increase in the number of young working people living at home between 1970 and 1996. More than half of all men and close to half of all women between the ages of eighteen and twenty-four were still living at home, and large numbers, particularly of

They have been called the revolving door generation.

men, continued living with parents into their thirties.[2] Many of those who do leave return at least once before they become established.

As young adults return home in increasing numbers, the phenomenon is studied by specialists from several different viewpoints: economic, social, psychological. Most young adults and many of their parents stress economics as the most important factor for remaining or returning home.

The increasing need for a college education in the late 1970s and early 1980s was matched by a steady movement away from outright grants for financing advanced education toward college loans. Although more middle-class parents were encouraging their children to seek higher education, few of us anticipated the astronomical increase in college costs that far outstripped the rise in our average incomes. Consequently more young people than ever before are beginning their twenties in serious debt. College loan payments begin six months after graduation, before many of them have managed to find decent jobs, reliable transportation, or a place to live.

The availability of credit cards to young people who would not have been eligible for any form of credit twenty years ago has added to their indebtedness. The credit card has become a standard requirement for much in today's young adult society, from buying gas at the pump to purchasing concert tickets over the phone. On many college campuses it is almost indispensable for functioning at all. The possibility of buying on credit hits older teens and young adults in their twenties where they are most economically vulnerable. It is part of the healthy idealism of youth to be filled with dreams and the accompanying unrealistic expectations of what can be accomplished beyond graduation. Credit cards invite them to gamble on those dreams, to incur debts that their limited incomes cannot meet. Credit provides the added illusion that the money in their pockets is discretionary, when it has, in fact, already been spent.

When gas required cash for purchase, everyone in the car dipped into their pockets and we went as far as that much gas allowed. We planned carefully or got stranded. Credit cards have removed the safety belts from our young adults. The only reality check comes with the bill at the end of the month.

The need to remain at home frequently does manifest itself as materialism, but all materialism is not necessarily rooted in laziness or greed.

The indebtedness of our young adults becomes even more crippling when they are faced with the escalating cost of housing. Despite a runaway economy and low unemployment, salaries at entry-level positions are simply not keeping pace with the housing market. In many middle-class communities, zoning has created financial ghettos by eliminating apartments and multifamily dwellings, keeping out not only the poorer families but also the young adults who grew up in the area. Many of these young people, particularly those who do not go on to college or who continue to live at home while attending college, choose jobs nearby but find themselves unable to find or maintain a home in the area. Some, whose lives have been more sheltered, express fear about living in the areas they *can* afford. Some have become single parents and return home with children they cannot care for while supporting themselves.[3]

At the same time, studies also indicate that some who stay home are, in fact, financially capable of being on their own and still choose not to be.[4] Cynics view this as proof of this generation's need to live in the comfort their parents took years to achieve. Those critics, who judge by their own growing up years and their remembered willingness to "do without," often fail to recognize that the conveniences of one generation become the necessities of the next.[5]

The need to remain at home frequently does manifest itself as materialism, but all materialism is not necessarily rooted in laziness or greed. Unlike teenagers, who view the luxuries their parents provide as their own fundamental right as household members, young adults returning home or remaining at home have often outgrown this attitude of entitlement. They are more apt to understand themselves as the recipients of their parents' hospitality than as their parents' responsibility. The emotional and social roots of their need to remain home and thus, of their delayed independence, extend far deeper than the need for material goods.

In the previous chapter we explored how we have become a people whose sense of self is based on our career, on what we do for a living, rather than on how we live. While "What do you do?" may have become the question by which we define one another and spell out identity in our society,[6] it is not the most basic human question. If we were to remove ourselves from the cocktail party setting, the business associates atmosphere, and place ourselves on vacation at a beach, on a plane or train journey, the first question we would ask in striking up an acquaintance would still be "What's your name?" But the second question in all likelihood would be, "Where are you from?"

Once we had the answer, we would begin to try to make connections. "I have an uncle whose wife's brother had a store in that state. Would it be anywhere near you?" "Where did you go to school, college, church? I knew someone who . . ." We want to connect in some way with the geography, the experiences, the place that has shaped the person so that we can begin to know who she or he is. This is such a universal experience that I suspect "Where are you from?" is one of the most basic human questions.

We may seek to define ourselves by what we do, but we have a fundamental desire to belong to a place, the need for a place called home. You see it in children playing tag. The first step, after everyone has shouted "Not it!" is to designate home base, a place where you are safe, where you can never be tagged out. Our instinctive play insists there must be a place where we can "go home" when we need time out to catch our breath.

> **We may seek to define ourselves by what we do, but we have a fundamental desire to belong to a place, the need for a place called home.**

Judeo-Christian revelation is filled with a God who calls us, like Abraham and Moses, not just out of the land of our ancestors but to a home that God will give us, into a land flowing with milk and honey. This longing for home is one of the desires most deeply rooted within us. Scripture makes it comparable to the desire for God.

I once traveled through the island of Cape Breton in Nova Scotia with a native, Sis MacNeil. Each time we were introduced, people immediately inquired if she was one of the "MacNeils of Sydney or the MacNeils of Margaree." Having clearly established her identity, they began to relate on a more intimate level, sharing stories about her family and ancestors, introducing her to ties they shared in common. I realized she was "known" in a way I never would be. This particular facet of identity, once common among us, is becoming extinct in most of our lives.

An increasingly national and global economy has created a mobile society where home is no longer the space we shared with our ancestors. Multinational corporations have relocated some of us all over the globe, while our highly acclaimed "frontier spirit" has pushed many others beyond the familiar paths of hometowns. Many adults in our country today have no sense of being "from" any place at all,[7] and in many ways, we have not grieved or even realized our loss.

Just as our mobile society has disconnected a sense of home from the land, the skyrocketing divorce rate has led to the disintegration of a sense of home rooted in primary relationships. Is it too far-fetched to suggest that perhaps today's youth stay home longer because it is no longer clear what constitutes "home" or how they will find or create it once they have left?

We are a people losing our sense of place, and, some sociologists suggest, attempting to fill the gap with what we own, with material things. We *create* our own homes.

We are a people losing our sense of place, and, some sociologists suggest, attempting to fill the gap with what we own, with material things. We *create* our own homes. This is part of the heritage we have bequeathed to this generation. For many of them, "home" has become the "stuff" we packed up and moved with them while we followed the career or the climate or the relationship, the things that remained present even when the people and the places changed. We offered them a home sometimes less dependent on *who* was in it than on *what* was in it. Is it any wonder they hesitate to leave home without some of those material things firmly in place? If home was never the three-bedroom house in which to grow up, it could still be the stereo or the teddy bear that always went along, creating a sense of place.

As our adult children struggle to establish apartments, we listen to talk of "making the place home," and know that they are not talking about sinking roots into a community, registering to vote, or finding a church, although these activities may have an important place in their lives. For them "home" itself has become far more immediate and personal. It means re-

Exploring the New Family

establishing the souvenirs, awards, special pictures, and knick-knacks that have adorned their rooms for years, shelving the books that have claimed permanent spots in their hearts, and creating the space for beloved pastimes and studies vital to their overall sense of well-being. While the "home" they left behind certainly included the town where they grew up, the house where they shared meals and chores, and the family itself, there was a deeper personal sense of ownership of their own private space. We were confronted with both that sense of ownership and the personal sense of loss in my son's reaction to our "takeover" of his long-empty bedroom.

It is always reassuring to know you can go home again. That's why I have to admit to feeling at least somewhat disconcerted when I heard the news that my parents would be ripping down the walls to my bedroom.

Sure, I haven't lived there in several years. And they were only talking about taking down one of the side walls, albeit the one with the Pink Floyd mural that I painted when I was in high school.

But the tiny room in the corner of my parents' basement would no longer be "my bedroom." Instead, Mom would use the expanded space for a much-needed home office.

Now when I visit my parents—or just stop off in Southbury for a respite on my way to somewhere else—I'll have to make do with a bed in one of my "sisters' rooms." (Of course, neither of them have lived there in a while, either.)

The old bunk bed that I used every night for years has been disassembled. The posters, trophies, and books that filled every nook have been packed away in anonymous boxes; they'll probably never again trigger memories about a certain rock concert or cross-country race. At least the mural was preserved, although it's tucked away with other forgotten arcana in the attic of my parents' garage.

In the years following my final departure from the house on Painter Road, I probably hadn't slept there any more than ten or fifteen nights a year. But when my former bedroom was transformed so abruptly to an office, an important physical link to my past was severed.

There's a lot more light coming into the room now that the number of windows has been doubled. The walls received a badly needed coat of paint, and the floors are covered with new carpeting.

To any sane observer, it's much more attractive. But for me, it's no longer home.

— JON, AGE TWENTY-NINE

When our youngest left for medical school, setting up her own apartment in the process, she begged us not to dismantle her room until she had graduated and had a chance to find her own "home." As I travel around the country, I frequently bump into the same phenomenon; young adults disturbed that a room they have not occupied for years has become a guest room or a study, and parents who are surprised and dismayed by their children's perception of encroachment.

Our generation grew up in an age of bigger families and smaller houses. Perhaps we never succeeded in staking out our private space to quite the same extent as our children did. Perhaps we did not need to. Our sense of home was far less dependent on *belongings* and far more dependent on *belonging:* to a family, a town, a community.

The musical *Carnival* begins with a young woman standing alone on stage, a battered suitcase on the floor beside her. She sings with longing of the small town where she grew up, the place where "everybody knows my name." The loneliness she expresses is not that far from the searching expressed by today's young adult; the difference is that she is able to name her own hunger.

"A place that's new is never cozy,
A room that's new is never sweet.
I want to have a chair that knows me
And walk a street that knows my feet
I'm very far from Mira now, and there's no turning
 back. . . ."[8]

There is no turning back, particularly no way to reclaim a past that many of us have never experienced. But the fact remains, we are talking about a "launching" stage in family life. It is difficult to "launch" from a less than firm foundation or from a base that is constantly in motion. Launching requires a solid center to push against. This is as true of the young adult as it is of everything from pole vaulters to rocket ships. As society continues to change, we may never again be a people with a sense of home rooted in a physical place. And the sense of home rooted in material belongings has become an economic obstacle on the road to maturity. Successfully launching this next generation may require finding ways beyond geography and possessions to establish firmer footings, other ways to claim a place as home.

Successfully launching this next generation may require finding ways beyond geography and possessions to establish firmer footings, other ways to claim a place as home.

THE COLLEGE HOUSING LOTTERY

Two girls lotteried last night for next year, and were disappointed to discover that they got a room facing the courtyard. They were both hoping for a nice Fifth Avenue room. Instead, they got ours. You can't see the Empire State building, or even New Jersey. You can't watch the sun set over our windowpane or count the stars on those quiet nights. You can't admire a skyline, or even a street sign.

But if you wake at just the right time, you can catch the sun creeping over the far building top. You can rise with the shadows.

If you sit at just the right angle, the ornate building positioned before our window looks like a great castle standing guard over all the city. We might even be fallen princesses locked in the dungeon waiting for our lost loves to save us.

And then there are the windows. Different sizes, shapes, depths. Openings to new worlds, or even other dimensions of our reality.

I tried to explain all about the friendly spirits that watch with us. About all the imagination games and the intellectual expansion possible in such a wonderful room.

They didn't quite understand, though they appreciated the grave effort. They left, all the more disappointed about missing out on a room with a view.

But what they didn't understand was that our window has a view, too. It may not be the *buena vista* they had their hearts set on. It may not be that which great photographers capture in moments. But it *is* a view.

It's funny how often we can miss out on such wonderful things thinking about what we could have had, instead of really looking at what we do have.

—LIZ, AGE NINETEEN

We need, in love, to practice only this:
letting each other go.
For holding on comes easily;
we do not need to learn it.

— **RAINER MARIA RILKE** [1]

Chapter 4
A SENSE
OF FAMILY

UNDERSTANDING the emotional and economic needs for remaining at home or returning home does not necessarily make the transition an easy one for parents or young adults. For those who remain home after high school, there is no definitive moment of separation, and the transition to postadolescence is more difficult for them and their parents. The patterns of adolescence have been strongly established, and in the absence of a clear breaking point, it can be difficult to move beyond them.

One young adult with whom we spoke had stayed home after high school while attending college. Presently thirty, married, and living in his own home, he still vividly remembers the difficulties of that period:

It felt like I was still in high school. Same old same old. A little more freedom, but not too much. I wanted more independence but had very little direction. Who knows what they truly want to do at eighteen? Would I have liked to be out on my own? Yeah. Did my parents want me out? Yeah. Could I afford it? No. I had more responsibility. I had to pay rent and have a job. My parents wanted me to be a middle-aged adult but treated me like a kid. And living there, I just couldn't figure out how to disconnect from them.

One mother with whom we spoke described her eighteen-year-old living at home after high school in the following manner:

> She knew we couldn't give her much, and she had always taken care of her own needs with odd jobs. The pattern just continued. She wanted to find someone to marry who would provide her with a home and allow her to become a stay-at-home mom. She felt like she didn't have a life of her own, and she was right, she really didn't.

In the not-too-distant past, families relied on physical distance to offer young adults the chance to move away from a parent-child relationship and into an adult friendship. The natural growth required simply by independent living fostered a different relationship by signaling the end of dependency. Successfully negotiating the transition out of adolescence requires finding ways to foster an interdependent adult relationship between parents and postadolescents who have not yet had the experience of living independently.

Returning home after college creates its own unique set of problems. Young adults have been "on their own," although frequently with parental support and at parental expense, for four or more years. While at school they answered to no one, other than professors, who were only concerned about classroom performance. Their personal space was theirs and could be maintained or not as they saw fit. Meals were at their own convenience, often made possible simply by the presentation of a meal card. Eating was not necessarily connected to cooking and cleaning up, or even to an awareness of those who did this portion of

Returning home after college creates its own unique set of problems.

the meal. Laundry may have been a more realistic task, but the presence of a large number of super-sized machines made the only inconvenience a personal one of time, not the communal one of sharing, common to family life.

Returning home can be disruptive and upsetting for both parents and young adults. Important changes have taken place during the years apart, changes not witnessed in daily life as they were happening, changes that may be hard for both to accept. Rules that once provided security and needed order in a family are seen as unnecessary and restrictive. Questions meant to express interest are frequently interpreted as nosy.

The tendency, both for young adults who remain at home and for those who return, is to go back to the familiar battle-grounds of adolescence. Adolescence focuses on separation and is a prelude to moving out. If postadolescence is going to be achieved within our families of origin, the focus must shift from separation to reintegration into an adult family.

Our three children all returned home after college. They worked, paid rent, and we all struggled to share space and respect privacy, but it wasn't easy for them or for us. Most of the problems were over small issues generally related to our caring too much and trying too hard, and invading their lives with our concern.

Typical of the time was an incident on a sunny June morning. Our twenty-two-year-old daughter was heading out the door to a friend's wedding in New Jersey. Her father, huddled over our battered Rand McNally road atlas and frustrated by the nonspecific directions her friend had supplied, was even more frustrated by our daughter's lack of attention to his well-meaning advice. Her journey would take her through New York City and over one of the infamous bridges. All she wanted to know was how long it would take. Her dad wanted her to understand the easiest and best way to negotiate the trip. As his frustration reached the level of belligerence, our young adult waltzed out the door.

"Why doesn't she listen? She is going to get lost again! I was trying to help."

I tried to calm him. It was her problem if she was late for the wedding, her responsibility to call friends and let them know she had decided to go straight to the wedding and not meet up with them first. If she lived somewhere else, we might not even have been aware of the trip. Because she was here, under our roof, we still felt compelled to protect her from problems. At times like this she resented our loving care, and I felt her frustration almost as deeply as my husband's.

This experience was just one of the many times when it would have helped to evaluate the consequences of the mistake before we insisted on helping to avoid it. What would have happened had she become lost? She was not going into the wilderness where her life would be in jeopardy. She was not going to be late for the most important job interview of her life, or even the job that might allow her to leave home. Perhaps in that situation we might have been able to claim a vested interest in her arriving on time. She was going to a wedding. It was her friend, her day. She took the little bit of advice she wanted, and we needed to let it go at that.

One of the greatest problems with postadolescents who live at home is that we are continually aware of their problems, decisions, anxieties, and failures.

One of the greatest problems with postadolescents who live at home is that we are continually aware of their problems, decisions, anxieties, and failures. They invade our space with general clutter, confusion, and constant motion. They invade our lives in the form of bad moods and acted out anger, frustration that is often leveled at us, though it has nothing to do with us. Our identity is so intimately connected with theirs, our happiness so dependent on theirs, it becomes difficult not to intervene, even though our attention may not be wanted, may not be needed, and may even be destructive.

I was easily as guilty of that type of intervention as my husband. Our children, who had the advantage of a dual-parent family for all their growing-up years, had the disadvantage of dual-parent worry as they entered postadolescence. Although they had paid their own bills since before they entered college, I worried all over again when the bills passed through my hands on the way to theirs. Although they were covering the costs of their phone calls, the late-night call to the friend in Germany kept me awake as it stretched beyond the thirty-dollar mark. I was certain they could not be aware of how long they had talked or what the bill was going to look like. At times like this my husband would gently remind me that if they consistently paid the bill, we had no reasonable complaint.

One reason for insisting our young people pay their own way, no matter how difficult that may be, is that it gives us less control over their choices. When a young adult is allowed to remain at home without sharing any of the expenses, it is easy for parents to resent the fact that their son or daughter has more "discretionary" money for movies, CDs, and trips than the parents themselves. Even when we sincerely wish they were saving a little more money toward their independence, it is far easier to accept how they choose to spend that money when it does not infringe on our needs.

For those who remain at home after high school, paying rent, sharing expenses, and perhaps even installing a separate phone line that is their total responsibility can be one way of

For those who remain at home after high school, paying rent, sharing expenses, and perhaps even installing a separate phone line that is their total responsibility can be one way of marking the beginning of a different, adult relationship with parents.

marking the beginning of a different, adult relationship with parents. "Payment in kind," doing chores in return for room and board, is not as successful as simple rent during this period.[2] This type of work sets the stage for familiar family battles over when a chore should be done, how it should be done, and who gets to decide when it is done properly. It carries heavy overtones of adolescence and fails to provide the first steps in independence. It puts parents back into the role of disciplinarian and enforcer, a role it is time to abandon.

Further complicating the issue is that when developing adults remain at home or young adults return home, it is not only *their* maturing that is affected by the decision. As parents we are also deprived of the distance that fosters successfully completing our own "moving on" stage of adult development.[3] Moving on requires letting go of the piece of our self-image we have invested so strongly in our children. One father, struggling with the letting go, and still phoning his three adult children faithfully every Sunday, confessed that by Sunday evening, he was as happy as the least happy of his children. "Moving on" means accepting not just our young adults' choices for how they earn and spend their money, the people they choose as friends and intimates, the careers and jobs they seek out and hold, but also accepting the mistakes and the unhappiness they bring on themselves, without letting it rob us of our own equanimity. This is one of the most difficult of all human tasks. It is the reason parenting is described at the beginning of this book as a terminal illness. The task is made much more difficult when the choices and problems are in front of us on a daily basis.

Successfully negotiating this stage depends on the ability of each person to assume his or her new role in a reconstructed adult family. Defining those roles is the task of the entire family. Beginning the task early—discussing finances, privacy, household space, and responsibility well in advance of high school graduation—can help in avoiding old dependency and caregiving roles in the postadolescent period.[4]

Discussing guidelines well in advance gives everyone a chance to grow into their new roles. It provides an opportunity to set reasonable limits on time and support before either becomes a personal issue. One father told his children before they finished high school that they would be given six months after completing their education to find a job. Then they would be charged one hundred dollars a month for the first year at home. Rent would double every year after that. He felt confident they would be gone before it reached eight hundred dollars.

Faced with a prolonged maturation that is no fault of their own, our children have the right to look to us for support as they journey through, but we also have the right, as parents, to look forward to a different, less demanding role in their lives, even if they are not yet ready to leave. Negotiating rules, roles, and responsibilities for this period, like much in family life, requires mutual respect and communication.

Successfully negotiating this stage depends on the ability of each person to assume his or her new role in a reconstructed adult family.

The fact remains that we are succeeding. On the whole this present generation of parents appears to have placed less value on independence and more value on interdependence than the generations that came before us. With that sense of interdependence, we are beginning to re-establish the concept of extended, healthy adult families.

Whether you view art as a reflection of life, or life as a reflection of art, the entertainment industry has become part of this movement. Two of the more popular prime-time television shows of the 1999–2000 season, *Judging Amy* and *Providence*, portray adults who have returned home and who have successfully established adult relationships in their homes. Even the popular *ER* has introduced parents and their relationships with their adult children as a critical part of the season's story line.

For the past decade, hit shows have focused on singles, living alone or with each other, pursuing a career in the city, being independent. The parents on these shows are often caricatures that provide laugh lines, significant in the lives of their young adults only in the ways they prevent them from living maturely and independently.

In both *Judging Amy* and *Providence*, the parents are established professionals, and so are the progeny. Both parents and children have lives of their own, but both are finding room in those lives for each other. Their new living arrangements contain enough stress to be believable but also infer a growing social acceptance for this new adult family.

Both shows have taken a new look at the intimacy versus commitment struggle that has separated the last two generations. But the hunger for intimacy is often viewed through the eyes of the older generation, the hunger for commitment through the younger. The reversal of roles hints at the insights communication might give us.

When Syd leaves home in *Providence*, her delighted father immediately turns her room into storage for his fishing gear.

Her experience in her new apartment reflects much of the modern search for home and family, with people proclaiming their independence but trying to recreate, in their group of tenants, the families they have left. The story, exaggerated for the sake of humor, is still a poignant commentary on the young adult's search for family in a world that longs for it at the same time that it denigrates those who cling to it.

Much of the growth of new adult relationships within a family today, in the absence of the physical space that once led to these, depends on a willingness to construct new spaces in our lives.

Syd worries, as so many of our own young adults do, if it is possible to go home when the childhood space that was hers no longer exists. She returns home to discover her family has created a new space for her. Much of the growth of new adult relationships within a family today, in the absence of the physical space that once led to these, depends on a willingness to construct new spaces in our lives.

Those spaces and how we go about creating them will differ from family to family and be highly dependent on what it meant to be a "child" within a particular home. How we define what it means to be an "adult" is usually done in contrast to our definition of "child." What do you perceive as the adult responsibilities in your home? What are the adult privileges? Defining these areas early gives everyone a place to begin the transition.

All examples limp because they are personal and limited by experience, but a few might help in beginning the discussion. If children in your home were not allowed to have computers, televisions, or phones in their rooms, young adults returning home can be encouraged to treat those same rooms as studio apartments, paying rent for them and having within them whatever their limited incomes can provide. If they can

A Sense of Family

afford a private phone line, it provides independence and frees parents from the roles of bill collector and telephone receptionist, both of which can cause constant friction. An answering machine becomes a great way of communicating with the young adult who is hard to pin down. Independent transportation (which can be anything from car, to bus, to car pool) is almost essential to the development of personal responsibility for one's job or education. No matter what ways they choose to create new space, parents must be ready and willing to surrender both responsibility and control for their young adults' lives, and young adults must find ways of claiming independence while living respectfully in another's space.

Looking back on our postadolescent time together, our middle child described it in this manner.

> I had very conflicting feelings. I wanted to be on my own. It was a letdown not to be at the point where I thought I should be, not having my own private space, having someone to answer to, not feeling free to just skip dinner, having the burden of knowing someone is worrying about you. I felt frustrated with not being in control of the space around me; my only individual space was my room.
>
> On the other hand, it gave me a sense of security. I had time to think about what I really wanted to do. It also gave me more of a sense of being part of a family than I had as a teenager. As you grow up, you think of what you want to be a part of, and that year at home helped me want to stay connected. If I had not come home it would have taken me a lot longer to reintegrate. I would have come home on major holidays. Not until I had children of my own, I think, or needed to take care of my parents would we have become friends. It is almost like I achieved

a certain maturity that would not have happened if I had not been home, kind of a sense of being an adult with my adult parents. We established a relationship that was more on the same level.

— BECKY, AGE TWENTY-SEVEN

The return of adult children to our homes is becoming an increasingly likely event. As our young adults are in need of more support, we parents have recognized the need and tried to respond in love. Our postadolescents, in turn, have struggled toward maturity in a situation that does not encourage it. We have both had to work at completing separation and achieving integration almost simultaneously.

The fact remains that we are succeeding. Many parents I meet in my travels admit to enjoying the presence of their young adults in their homes. Many of the young adults with whom my son and I spoke have established healthy friendships with their parents, confiding in them and seeking their advice far more than ever before. Parents we interviewed acknowledged this relationship as radically different from the relationship they shared with their own parents. For many it is a surprising benefit of this extended period of maturation. As Becky pointed out, it offers the possibility of an adult friendship that might otherwise take years to achieve.

We awake
On a tilting, spinning sphere
Racing around a star
Hurtling through a galaxy
Accelerating through a universe
And our enlightened psyche
Longs
For the stability
Of a flat earth.

Chapter 5
A SENSE
OF SECURITY

THE TALK at the East Coast Conference focused on the mythical "Generation X," and several of the parents gathered around one of the publisher's booths to share war stories. One mother shared with the other parents how she had reached her wits' end with her high-spirited daughter. The daughter's risk-taking capacity far outweighed her mother's ability to let go. When the young woman left for college, with its greater risks and more serious consequences, the mother decided it was time for a lecture.

Trying to impress on her daughter the tremendous freedom and opportunity she had been given, the mother said the one thing all of us promise ourselves we will never say: "When I was your age . . ." Once started she couldn't stop. Her daughter heard all about her mother's college life where there simply were no coed dorms, where every visitor had to check in with a matron at the front desk, where visitors had to be out by ten, and a campus curfew made sure everyone was safely inside at a certain time.

When the mother stopped to take a breath, she realized she had committed the unforgivable sin and waited for her daughter's derision or, at the very least, indifference. To her surprise, the young **"You must have felt so safe."** woman was quiet for a moment then responded wistfully, "You must have felt so safe."

Several weeks later, I was heading to a conference in Los Angeles. Paranoid traveler that I am, I arrived at the airport ninety minutes before takeoff, only to be told there might be a problem in giving me a seat. My ticket was in my hand; I was early. How could I not have a seat?

The fog that had blanketed L.A. overnight had caused the cancellation of two earlier flights. All those people were trying to fit on the little 737 parked at Gate 1 at Bradley International. Some of them were being given high priority. My own contract for the conference had to be seen by a manager before I was also given priority status and a seat on the plane. In Chicago the scene was repeated with half the time, twice the number of people, and triple the frustration.

Arriving in Los Angeles, I called the limo company with whom I had made a reservation. They informed me that although they required reservations, they never actually came to the airport until the plane landed and the traveler called. It would be about forty-five minutes before they could get there. Disgusted, I hung up and took the first shuttle I found. If they were not going to honor my reservation, neither was I.

At the hotel, check-in was the first event of the day that went smoothly. The person at the desk took the key card, ran it through the machine that imprints it, and gave me my room number. I arrived at the room, exhausted, opened the door, and found someone else in it.

In one day I had a ticket that was not a ticket, a reservation that was not a reservation, and a key that was not really a key. I grew up in a time when a ticket was a ticket. It meant you could get on the train or the merry-go-round or whatever it was the ticket promised you. It was real. Keys were made of metal, and when you had them, no one else could. A simple reality like metal keys, I suspect, offered us a sense of stability, a reliability of certain elements in life. Some things could just be counted on.

This world of nothing stable, nothing permanent, very little you can be sure of is the only world the current generation has known. They have grown up on quicksand, children of adults who grew up on bedrock. Our information was stored in books that ran the risk of growing moldy. Information today is stored in computers, subject to viruses, worms, crashes, and total annihilation. As children of the cold war, we held air raid drills. One blast from the horn meant we had time to get to the basement and line up against the walls on our knees, arms over our heads. Two blasts meant there was no time; crouch down under the desk and cover your head. But we were always offered the possibility of surviving the bomb. Our children were given no such illusions.

This world of nothing stable, nothing permanent, very little you can be sure of is the only world the current generation has known.

We waded in streams that we believed would always be there, climbed trees we thought were immortal, and took clean air for granted. Our children were taught that the aerosol cans that contained their hair spray were destroying the ozone layer over Antarctica, the paper napkins and paper towels that had become staples of life were depleting the rain forests, and the very air they breathed and water they drank were endangered.

When the Berlin Wall came down in 1989, my husband and I were stunned by the reaction of our seventeen-year-old. We were all overjoyed, but her joy bordered on hysteria. It was not until years later that she was able to articulate the deep roots of her reaction.

I remember, from age eight to twelve, I was terrified we would all die in a nuclear war. The political climate between the Soviet Union and us (even though I would not have been able to describe it as such back then) seemed so unstable and frightening. The news every night was filled with so much explicit turmoil, it was all around all the time. Every night I prayed that the war would not happen. Perhaps that is how I developed my exaggerated fear of death.

I sensed a lack of control over life. I had no influence over what might happen. It seemed like a loss of innocence. Any child should feel safe, and it was a loss of security. My parents couldn't protect me from it, and I assumed everyone was afraid like me.

By the time I was a teenager, I knew the unlikelihood of nuclear war because I realized the United States would not pursue a course that would result in total annihilation. I began to understand how interdependent we really are.

Environmentally I became aware of how our actions affect other people. I took the earth personally. Politically I became interested in other nations and how our actions as a country affect other people, not just other nations. It brought me to where I am now, wanting to help others, feeling a sense of responsibility. I am not only responsible to myself, but to my community and to my world.

— BECKY, AGE TWENTY-SEVEN

This is an insecure generation raised in an insecure, volatile world. It stands to reason that their period of launching will be more anguished and prolonged. At the same time, I suspect the mercuric nature of our lives has also influenced the many ways this generation is in a rush. The world is slipping out of control, and they are in a hurry to grasp at everything. We blame ourselves for their need for instant gratification. We believe it is because we have been too willing, too eager to give them everything they wanted, all the things we did not have. Certainly this is part of the problem. But maybe their need is based not only on our willingness to give them everything we can but also on our inability to promise them a future.

Time once moved more slowly. We were content in a simpler age to measure it by the earth's rotation and the sun's position in the sky. It was a vast, astronomical concept, relating us to the two largest bodies that ordered our universe. Our watches had faces that showed the relation of every moment to the ones that came before and the ones that would follow after. But time is no longer measured in seconds and minutes as the earth rotates. Time is measured by the revolution of an electron, the smallest body, and it has been subdivided into nanoseconds. Our children have grown up with digital watches and digital clocks, clocks that have no past or future. The only moment they know is the present one.

Altering the basic concept of time must surely affect our sense of self in relation to the world. It may not be the cause of our present sense of urgency, our need to fit more into every day than we once would have attempted in a week, but it must have some effect on it.

This generation has grown up with this urgency, with lives tightly scheduled from preschool onward, between lessons, school, and organized sports. Seven years ago, when our youngest was sixteen years old, she was asked to write an essay addressing what she perceived to be the greatest problem facing the world today. In her eyes the world's most serious problem was the loss of childhood. The inability of children to imagine, the lack of time for free play, the loss of backyard games and family stories, isolation into peer groups away from the influence of other caring adults, all of this she characterized as destructive to the most basic element of a healthy society—a healthy childhood.[1] Have we been so intent on providing all that was necessary for our children to become competent adults that we have denied them the childhood they needed to experience before they could leave it behind?[2]

Have we been so intent on providing all that was necessary for our children to become competent adults that we have denied them the childhood they needed to experience before they could leave it behind?

Childhood has been further limited by a world in which violence has become a primary coping skill. Even if crime had not invaded our children's neighborhoods, it invaded their homes through the media. In my childhood only the bullies got into fights, and they could usually be avoided. In this generation's childhood, and even more so for those presently in elementary school, the bullies have guns and no one is safe. If this generation seems a little jaded at times, it may only reflect that they lost their innocence far too early.

Illness represents an even greater fear for this generation than it did for us at their age. Time moves so much faster, and time is money. The loss of time becomes more critical. Coupled with that is the reality that as a nation we are experiencing a health care deficit.[3] There are cuts in social services, and home health care workers are impossible to find. Hospitals send people home twenty-four hours after surgery to recover on their own. But no one is there to nurse them. A majority of all mothers work outside the home; many are single parents with no other means of support. They simply cannot risk getting ill because there is no one to care for them.

Personal instabilities are played against the economic backdrop of the most volatile stock market in history. World news reflects a cautious, tentative peace but fails to offer a genuinely hopeful vision of the future. Constant talk of global warming reminds us of the fragility of the ecosphere even as El

Niño wreaks havoc with the weather, and drought plagues huge portions of our country and the world. New findings in medicine race against new diseases and new strains of resistant bacteria.

Perhaps what is most amazing and most hopeful amid this escalating uncertainty is that the insecurity in which this generation has been raised has *not* led to an increase in suicides among the postadolescent population. The trend appears to be just the opposite. For young people aged twenty to thirty, the National Center for Health Statistics[4] shows a substantial decline in the number of suicides from 1980 through 1996. The minor decrease in overall population of this age-group during that period is not enough to negate the significance of this trend. Although it does not rule out in any way serious emotional problems faced by this age-group, it simply suggests that they are growing less susceptible to being overcome by despair.

Parents we interviewed gave us the first hint of this developing resilience.

Parents we interviewed gave us the first hint of this developing resilience. The parents themselves spoke of being somewhat disconcerted by the equanimity with which their young adults treated a reversal of fortunes that necessitated returning home. For us at their age such a return represented failure. For them it was more apt to be viewed as a bump in the road. Having the rug ripped out from under you is proving to be not quite as unsettling when life has already taught you that nothing is stationary.

In that same vein, the sudden derailing of a career is proving not as troubling to a generation that never quite succeeded in identifying themselves with what they do. The job uncertainties that accompany the rapidly changing marketplace appear to be teaching them to place their sense of security and identity less in specific employment and more in their general employability.[5]

The knowledge of troubling world conditions with which they are continually bombarded, far from paralyzing them, has led to their increased level of volunteerism.[6] Robert Putnam, who explores the increasing isolationism of Americans in *Bowling Alone,* reports volunteerism rising in only two groups in our country, seniors and nineteen- to twenty-five-year-olds. Yet his point about the isolationism of the age still holds true for post-adolescents. As there is with their faith, which we explore in chapter 7, there is an individualism in their volunteering. No single major issue, like civil rights or the Vietnam war, draws them together and orients them to action, and so they are far less visible than their predecessors of the sixties and seventies. Yet volunteer agencies report a quiet increase in their numbers. They are building playgrounds, caring for the environment, running exercise programs for the elderly and after-school programs for the young, without any of the angered frenzy or fanfare that marked so much of their parents' age of idealism.

The parents of today's young adults rebelled against a world that "had always been that way," a church that "always did it that way," social norms that appeared to us to be so stable that they were stagnant. Today's young adults struggle to discover stable ground as they hang on to the remnants of whatever security they can find in a world that is changing so fast that nothing is ever the same.

Webster's Collegiate Dictionary offers two different definitions for *insecure.* The first describes insecure as "subject to fears, doubts, etc.; not confident or assured." Its synonym is instability, and it indicates a lack of poise or self-confidence. The second definition is, "not safe, exposed or liable to risk or danger."[7] Its synonym is vulnerability. In discussing this generation's sense of security it is important to keep the distinction in mind. This generation is far more vulnerable than it is unstable. Its exposure to the risks and dangers of an insecure world has not produced less assured or less competent adults. But it has definitely contributed to the lengthening of the process by which they reach confident adulthood.

"Is God a grown-up or a parent?"

Five-year-old eyes,
Raised searchingly to mine,
You question.

Baffled by what thought
Could have raised
This enigma,
I offer you
A question of my own.

"Is there a difference
Between being a grown-up
And being a parent?"

"Oh yes, Mommy."

Assurance fills your voice,
As the puzzlement fades
From your eyes.
This truth you know.

"Grown-ups love you when you are good,
And parents love you anyway."

Chapter 6

A SENSE
OF FORGIVENESS

I MET a young man named Noah during his junior year at Harvard. He spoke of never having received a failing grade until he was in college. Stunned, I asked him how he had managed to get that far without failing.

He explained that he had been sent to exclusive prep schools where children were never graded. They received only positive comments on their report cards. Slightly incredulous, I had inquired, "There was never anything in the whole of school that you were told you weren't good at?"

He grinned ruefully and recounted a brief story. In sixth grade he had been required to take chorus, despite being totally tone deaf. Even the eleven-year-old Noah had recognized the stretch when his teacher wrote on his report card, "Sings best when accompanied by a very large group."

We raised a generation in the seventies and eighties that was not allowed to experience failure. We wanted to protect their self-esteem. What we failed to understand was that self-esteem cannot be taught. Trying to teach it is like trying to teach someone balance before they learn to ride a bike. You learn to ride, and you acquire balance along the way, discovering your own center of equilibrium. You learn that you are capable and responsible by behaving in capable and responsible ways, and that is how you develop self-esteem. It is not taught; it is earned.

What our children acquired from the educational effort was not self-esteem but a fear of failure, and along with that the belief they were not acceptable if they failed. If we can't fail, we can never be forgiven.

What our children acquired from the educational effort was not self-esteem but a fear of failure, and along with that the belief they were not acceptable if they failed.

Several years ago when I was directing a parish program in religious education, I was asked by a third-grade teacher if I would come in to do a lesson on forgiveness for children preparing for the sacrament of Reconciliation. I planned the lesson, went into the class, and began by asking, "How many of you have ever made a mistake?" Not one child in that entire class of eighteen had ever made a mistake! My lesson demolished, I turned to the teacher and said, "I think I had better come back next week."

I spent the week trying to understand the phenomenon I had just witnessed, and decided, eventually, that what I needed was a song. I found a Sesame Street song in which Big Bird assures us that everyone makes mistakes—moms and dads, sisters and brothers—everyone. We don't have to get sad or mad, we just have to start over. We will still be loved just as much as before "we spilled the milk all over the floor." I brought the record and a small record player into the third-grade class.

When the song had finished, I asked the children again if anyone had ever made a mistake. Either it had been a very busy week for eight-year-olds in our town, or the class finally felt safe, because everyone in the class had made a mistake. In our educational focus on self-esteem, we have lost an environment where "everyone makes mistakes" and it is okay because it can be forgiven.

Exploring the New Family

If the prodigal son in Luke's Gospel returned home today, it would have to be with a swagger and a demonstration of how liberated he had become. Would his parents find it necessary to brag to others about all the great experiences he had had while he was gone? Would the elder son feel more than the simple rage expressed in the story at how easily forgiveness was given? Would he instead feel the compulsion to go out and do likewise rather than feel belittled by his brother's adventurous spirit? Have we created a society in which it is not safe to admit you are wrong, and every action must have some type of justification? It has always been difficult to admit our mistakes. But for this generation, we have made it almost impossible.

Society has made it almost as difficult to offer forgiveness as it is to ask for it. We are warned in many situations that forgiving the offender condones the offense. It is certainly true that our stock response to "I'm sorry," the usual, "That's all right," does indeed condone the behavior. It states that it was "all right." But that is not the same as forgiveness. To tell someone, "I forgive you" infers that what he or she did was not okay. The fact that what the person did requires forgiveness implies that it was indeed wrong, perhaps even sinful. Even though we know this, we are willing to offer forgiveness and give the person the opportunity to make amends. This gesture does not take responsibility away from the offender, but rather lays it squarely on the offender's shoulders.

Those who have had little opportunity to receive forgiveness have had little chance to learn how to offer it in a way that does not sanction the offense. Forgiveness is often portrayed as offering one an

Those who have had little opportunity to receive forgiveness have had little chance to learn how to offer it in a way that does not sanction the offense.

invitation to hurt us again. But not forgiving does not control the behavior of another. If that person desires to hurt us again, he or she probably will, whether or not we have forgiven him or her. In choosing *not* to forgive, it is *our* behavior that is being controlled. We are allowing whatever evil was done to us to control us and our response. Not to forgive seldom hurts our enemies and almost always destroys us, allowing the evil to gain power over us. When Jesus told us to love our enemies, it was not simply because he loved our enemies, but because he loved us.

The ability to grant forgiveness and the ability to admit you are wrong and ask forgiveness are essential to emotional maturity. Accepting responsibility for our own actions begins with the development of the moral emotions: empathy, shame, and guilt. Empathy makes its appearance first. Even babies are capable of showing concern for a child or adult who is obviously distressed. Shame, first manifested between the ages of eighteen months and two years, is the ability to feel embarrassment when we are caught doing something we were trusted not to do. Guilt, the internalization of shame and the ability to feel bad even if we are not caught, follows at about age three.[1]

In our society the development of the moral emotions has been endangered. Today's young adults were overburdened as little children with so much violence in the form of entertainment that many have turned off their empathy in self-defense. Shame and guilt were bad words in a culture intent on teaching children to feel good about themselves at all costs. Shame became confused with humiliation, and guilt with the inability to let go of past mistakes. Truthfully, however, guilt is one of the things that ultimately enables us to let go and move on. What we are culpable for, we are capable of changing. We can ask forgiveness and be freed to behave differently. We can make amends and try to right the wrong or at least make restitution. Without the acceptance of our own responsibility and our own guilt, there can be no forgiveness, no sense that we are free to behave differently. Without an awareness of our own failings, it becomes difficult to forgive the failings of others or to trust them to behave differently.

Nobel laureate Wislawa Zimborska, in a wonderful poem called "In Praise of Feeling Bad About Yourself," points out that only the human animal is capable of shame and guilt. Feeling bad for what we have done is a sign of our humanity. A clear conscience, according to Zimborska, can be the sign of bestiality.

Asking and offering forgiveness is a learned skill, one that requires practice in small areas before we are capable of using it in larger ones. Dismissing the wrongdoing and the failures of young children deprives them of an opportunity to learn that mistakes do not intrinsically damage who they are. Then, as young adults, they will find it difficult to accept the consequences of their own actions. If the skill has not been acquired in childhood, it still can and should be fostered in postadolescence.

Accepting responsibility for their own failings is essential for young adults to be able to separate from their family of origin. Blaming parents, grandparents, or siblings for all that has gone wrong in their lives is another way of remaining dependent on them. It implies that one's family still has control. Helping our young adults to see that blaming others **Accepting responsibility for their own failings is essential for young adults to be able to separate from their family of origin.** for our difficulties only keeps us trapped within them is a tenet that must be modeled by parents before it can be spoken with any true authority.

All parents have failed, some atrociously. Those children who cannot forgive find it difficult to move on with their own lives. Without forgiveness it is hard not to be governed by anger and bitterness. Every action becomes a reaction to what has been done to us.

All children have failed, some atrociously. Parents who cannot forgive are unable to let go of past mistakes. Our "buttons" are easily pushed. We are angered by incidents that may be innocuous in themselves but hold too many overtones of past failures and rebellions. Without forgiveness it is difficult to respond to the present instead of reacting to the past.

Forgiving one another for the failures of both parents and children in the growing up process is essential if we are ever to achieve reintegration. None of us can change the past. Every parent has moments that are deeply regretted, and most young adults also have incidents they wish had never happened. Being continually confronted with them and reminded of the past hurt reopens wounds that need to be healed for a truly adult friendship to blossom.

Sometimes in the young adult family some of the hurts have gone too deep and have been allowed to fester too long. We know each other so intimately, we are capable of hurting each other quite deeply, and some of us have. We no longer know where to begin. The hurt seems beyond our ability to forgive. At this point the story of the prodigal son offers us a solution. When the elder son is unable to forgive, the father tells him, "All that I have is yours." I don't think he is referring just to the farm or the inheritance. I think he is talking about *his* forgiveness. When we are unable to forgive on our own, we are invited to entrust the hurt to God's forgiveness. We do not have to feel forgiveness. All that is required of us is that we *act* with mercy.

The very term *mercy* implies something the other does not deserve. Justice gives the other what is rightfully his. When a court requires a criminal to repay the people he has robbed, that is justice. When a governor grants pardon to a convicted killer on death row, that is called an act of mercy. Mercy gives more than the other has the right to expect. To act with mercy is to acknowledge that we have been hurt beyond our own ability to forgive. The hurt is so great that it does not deserve our forgiveness. But rather than be trapped in the pain, we are entrusting it to God. We are not "forgetting" or allowing the other to hurt us again. We are choosing to act benevolently.

When we are unable to forgive on our own, we are invited to entrust the hurt to God's forgiveness.

Many of us who are now parents of young adults grew up in a generation that was burdened with unhealthy guilt. We wanted to free our children from that burden, to have a healthier sense of themselves. We may have forgotten that true freedom is found in forgiveness. The integration stage of postadolescence offers us the opportunity to forgive the past and create a future no longer bound by its hurts.

The windowpane is old, and the glass, blurred with age; the sun is blinding and the shade beckons to cool the afternoon's scorch but i sit, transfixed by a view i can't even see.

   i know there is an ocean: i've heard it some hours beckoning young lovers, calming bitter souls, lulling the world with its quiet tides.

   i know there is a forest: dark and inviting. i have sensed its watchful eyes and have been sheltered by its velvet branches. i have eaten its wild berries and have sung with its hungry wolves.

   i know there is a desert: dry and barren. i have tasted its loneliness and followed its hopeful mirage; i have drunk from its dry rivers and seen the beauty of its hidden life.

     i know there is a night
     i know there is a moon
     and stars
   but it's all about faith, isn't it?

   trusting that inner knowledge that there is something beyond the windowpane;
   that the window is not the view . . . sometimes
   so we all rock in our chairs
   and the shadows change,
   and we are shaken by a world that, at times, doesn't even feel like it's moving.

—LIZ, AGE TWENTY

Chapter 7

A SENSE
OF THE SACRED

IF YOU travel Interstate 90 between Albany and Rochester, New York, on the north side of the highway you will discover a rusty, abandoned bridge standing starkly in the middle of the Mohawk River. The small dam at the base of the bridge, which once supplied power for the area mills, is no longer connected to any generators. The bridge itself no longer reaches either shore. It ends abruptly, about twenty feet from the riverbanks, a useless anomaly marring a peaceful landscape.

Religion, at its best, is a bridge designed to connect the ordinary with the sacred. Its rituals, its prayers, its ancient wisdom and faith stories are all meant to offer easier access to the holy. When we become too absorbed in the bridge, in designing, rebuilding, decorating, deciding the rules for who can use it, we have lost sight of its primary purpose. Too often in our history as a church we have become so focused on the bridge itself that we have lost sight of the riverbanks.

For many postadolescents, religion resembles the abandoned Mohawk River bridge along I-90. It does not touch either shore. It has little connection with their reality, and it fails to satisfy their longing for the sacred. Its "disconnection" prevents religion from being a source of energy in their lives. It is not

Religion, at its best, is a bridge designed to connect the ordinary with the sacred.

much more than an interesting anomaly that might be worth exploring on a Sunday afternoon when there is little else to do.

Many parents who approach me as I travel want to talk about the reality that their children no longer go to church. The parents' difficulty is not that their young adults aren't attending, but with their own guilt over a reluctance to try to bring them back. We recognize in our almost-adult off-spring much of what we once refused to acknowledge in ourselves. The questions are often the ones we had but never voiced; the challenges frequently reflect those that obedience kept at bay in our own lives. We relate to their struggle; at times we even envy their freedom. "Will our children have faith?" is no longer the question. Everything from national polls and surveys to intimate family conversations assures us that they are people of faith.[1] They have not rejected God; they are rejecting church.

They have not rejected God; they are rejecting church.

Those of us who are Catholic, and whose childhood and teen years were intercepted by the Second Vatican Council, grew up with a strongly ritualized, controlling religion. Conversations with God involved the use of church-approved formulas, the content of the conversation dictating the choice of formula. I have a vivid memory of myself at eight suggesting to a Protestant friend that we should say a Hail Mary to Saint Anthony to help us find a library book she had lost. "Why," she asked incredulously, "would you say a Hail *Mary* to Saint *Anthony?*" It was a prayer, the only one I knew that I thought might work under the circumstances.

We raised our own children with the new fruits of spirituality and prayer that the Second Vatican Council had given us. We encouraged them to read the Scriptures. We taught them that they could pray in their own words, that they did not need an intermediary or a formula to be able to approach God, and

Exploring the New Family

they believed us. We shared with them our new social consciousness.

Many of us were children of the fifties, before the civil rights movement, before justice became a moral issue in the church. It was not that we were particularly prejudiced; most of us were simply ignorant. I remember visiting Washington, D.C., as a child and asking what "black crow" motels were. When my mother explained that they were for the "Negroes," the acceptable term of the time, my naive response was, "Why don't they want to stay with us?"

Our children would never have made such a mistake. They were born post–Martin Luther King Jr. and the great civil rights movement. We taught them what Pope Paul VI taught us: faith that does justice. Many of them were not allowed to mow lawns at country clubs that discriminated against African Americans, Jews, or any other group of people because of their race or religion. They grew up to challenge the church in ways many of us would never have dreamed of challenging it. They did it partly because we had taught them to be just and partly because we had taught them they could reach out to God on their own. And when the church refused to listen, they simply jumped into the river and swam.

We are the generation who fought for possession of the bridge, for changes in the way it was structured and administered, for a more open approach to all it represented. When I was in fifth grade, I challenged the Sister who taught me that unbaptized babies went to Limbo. I insisted that there could not be a place of perfect happiness without God and refused to back down from my position, even when it meant detention. If you were to discuss Limbo with a young adult today, he or she would not challenge or argue but would simply dismiss the idea, saying casually, "I respect your right to believe that, but I certainly don't." For those of us who fought so hard for the bridge, this gentle disregard can be most painful.

It is not that our young adults are not spiritual. Although some of their favorite television shows betray their obsession with the total absurdity of life *(Ally McBeal),* others, like *The X-Files,* reflect a search for the mystical if not the religious. Even *Ally* is not afraid to tackle the issues of mechanically prolonging life and of suicide by choice, while *The X-Files* delves not only into aliens but also stigmata and speaking in tongues. Ayn Rand's book *Fountainhead,* with its exploration of total self-involvement and aggrandizement, shares young adults' best-seller lists with the *Celestine Prophecy,* a parable proclaiming a spiritual way of life.

As part of their quest for the sacred in life, young adults are seeking spiritual directors in greater numbers than any group in history. The increase in their volunteerism, noted earlier, in services ranging from soup kitchens to literacy campaigns, is yet another aspect of their attempt at lived faith. But although their faith prays and "does justice," it fails to seek a community to celebrate ritual. They have imbibed the actions of faith but rejected the religion that was meant to support and nourish those actions.

Today's young adults have lost the sense of need for a communal set of beliefs, a communal celebration of faith, a communal sign and symbol. Although it is certainly possible for them to jump into the river and swim, or even to build simple rafts on a cultic type of spirituality, it limits the numbers they can bring with them. This individualized faith journey reflects the individualized culture of the eighties and nineties that gave it birth. It leaves nothing behind, no stable bridge, no opportunity for others to connect the spiritual with their ordinary existence.

When Mother Teresa and Princess Diana died on the same day, the outpouring of love for Diana disturbed many of our generation, puzzled by the precedence given her death. Diana's goodness had been completely individual, a kind of "personal sacred." As such it died with her. Part of the commemoration, the adulation, that followed her death was the need to acknowledge her goodness and to commemorate all that we had lost through her death. Mother Teresa's goodness belonged to all, a communal sacred that survives in the body of the church, in all who emulate her lifestyle, support her efforts, and remain attentive to her admonitions.

The communal sacred is in danger in this generation, and part of the blame rests with our generation. We have at times been guilty of hiding behind the "communal good," allowing someone else to live the "holy life" for us while we financially supported their endeavors, claiming for ourselves the sacrifices of the "Body of Christ" without ever surrendering any of our own comfort. The great prophetic voice of this generation challenges us to count not only on our saints, but to live out the holiness ourselves.

Revelation has a tendency to challenge us where we are most comfortable. When the canon of sacred Scripture was first defined, it was not the texts the church omitted as apocryphal that was most surprising. What was truly amazing was the texts the church kept and declared as authentic revelation. We kept two totally different Creation stories, two different accounts of the conquest of Canaan, four different Gospels with opposing accounts of many things from the Nativity to the Last Supper, the Resurrection, and the gifts of the Spirit. We not only kept these accounts, we also said they were all *true*. We not only said they were true, we also said they were *inspired*. Our sacred Scriptures make it abundantly clear that as a church we believe it is possible for differing communities to perceive the same truth differently, and yet both are still true. Both can be inspired revelation.

Perhaps that belief has something to say to us about this generation. Perhaps theirs is a different gospel, another perception of truth, and our own sacred canon will not be complete without theirs.

Most of us who grew up overshadowed by the activity of Vatican Council II tend to identify with the Gospel of Luke. We like the Emmaus story and plan countless classes and education conferences around it. But if truth be told, I suspect that as Capuchin priest and author Michael Crosby[2] suggests, we are more the Gospel of Matthew. Most of us would have real difficulty with many of the people in Luke. An easy example is the widow who gives her last cent to the Temple (Luke 21:14). Our common sense says she should have used it to feed her family. We struggle with Lazarus and the rich man (Luke 16:19–31). We would probably not give Lazarus the scraps from our table either; we would clean him up and help him find a job. The prodigal son (Luke 15:11–31) raises all kinds of questions in our minds: What did he do after he was home for a couple of weeks and had grown accustomed to hot meals and clean sheets? What about the older brother who had been doing his younger brother's share of the work and bearing the brunt of his parents' grief? We are more comfortable with Matthew's story of the unforgiving debtor whose master forgave him his debt, but when the servant refused to forgive another servant, rose up in rage and exacted punishment (Matt. 18:23–35).

Most of us who grew up overshadowed by the activity of Vatican Council II tend to identify with the Gospel of Luke.

Matthew wrote for a community emerging into middle class, a community in the process of developing a hierarchical church, our community. The one Scripture quote most Catholics of my generation can finish is, "You are Peter, and on this rock I will build my church, and the gates of Hades will not prevail against it" (Matt. 16:18).

But this generation's spirituality is far removed from Matthew. They have no need for the genealogies of Matthew and Luke, no need for carefully grounding Jesus in his family and in his historical and geographic setting. They begin by jumping off into the mystical. "In the beginning was the Word, and the Word was with God" (John 1:1). Theirs is the Gospel of John. Like John, they jump into the water and swim.

Theirs is the Gospel of John. Like John, they jump into the water and swim.

A careful reading of the Gospel of John suggests an image of Jesus different from the synoptics, an image often more in keeping with the struggles of today's postadolescent. We know them as an uprooted generation longing for a sense of place and searching for home. They are not likely to leave everything behind to follow the Lord, as the disciples do in all three synoptic Gospels. A Messiah who says that, "foxes have holes, and birds of the air have nests; but the Son of Man has nowhere to lay his head"(Matt. 8:20), is not issuing a call that will resonate in their hearts. Discipleship in John holds out a different promise. It is the disciples who approach Jesus, and it is Jesus who asks, "What do *you* want?" They respond with the question that is at the core of so much of the searching of today's young adults, "Master, where do you live?" He says, "Come and see," and they go to his home and spend the day.

Discipleship is not the only thing that begins "at home" in John. In the synoptics the first miracle happens in the

A Sense of the Sacred

synagogue. For Mark and Luke it is the curing of the man with the unclean spirit. Matthew does not actually tell us about the first miracle; he simply says that Jesus was teaching in the synagogues and curing the sick, implying the synagogue setting. Only in John does the first miracle happen at a home. And Jesus is not curing the sick, forgiving sin, or raising the dead in John's advent of the public ministry. He is turning water into wine for a family party. Not only that, he is doing it for his mother! (John 2:1–11).

The hunger for justice so characteristic of today's young adult also finds a particular place in John. Although the cleansing of the Temple happens in all four Gospels, in the synoptics it happens at the end of the public ministry of Jesus. He teaches first and then calls to justice and holiness. Only in John does it happen at the beginning (John 2:13–25).

When I read this passage today, I tend to think of the Temple as the body, both my own and the Body of Christ. I suspect this reflects childhood learning on the body as the temple of the Holy Spirit, but it also colors the way I understand this passage. If the temple is the body, then who are the money changers who are violating the Body of Christ? What are the sins committed by the church and in the church against the Body of Christ, sins which awake in Jesus such rage? I suspect this generation, with its highly developed sense of justice, will begin rather than end its religious journey by driving out anyone or anything that would violate the temple. Their first communal religious act may well be to challenge any injustice committed against the Body of Christ, injustice based on the body, on gender, on disability, on sexual orientation, on sex itself. If we invite them in, we must be ready for them to overturn the tables before they even get through the door. If they frustrate us with their inability to wait for justice, when their impatience borders on intolerance, refusing to accept how long it takes for a massive, hierarchical church to change, then we must remember who taught them this profound sense of justice. We did, the community of Matthew.

Those of us raised on the Baltimore Catechism question-and-answer rote approach to a carefully memorized "deposit of faith" are troubled by the spirituality of a generation that lacks solid grounding and appears to exhibit little desire to learn. Our attempts to involve them in classes and in young adult ministry limp badly, and that is in those communities that are still trying. It is not their desire that is lacking, but rather our models for tapping that desire.

Two of my three children went to the same college in Connecticut. On the campus there is a long hill overlooking the Connecticut River. Any warm morning between the hours of midnight and four a.m. you will find the hill peopled with young adults on blankets, with cheap wine and cheese. Many are simply enjoying one another as young people have for centuries. But far more than I would have ever expected are engrossed in profoundly spiritual discussions, sharing thoughts we never considered until long after college. These same students welcomed us parents to cozy wine and cheese gatherings in run-down rented quarters on the back streets surrounding the campus. And when the late-night conversations inevitably turned to faith, to cosmology, to belief in the future, it was the parents who lapsed into uncomfortable silence.

In John's Gospel Nicodemus comes to Jesus by night (John 3:1–21). They sit and talk all night, no doubt with a bottle of cheap wine and a loaf of bread between them. I see my own young adults in the searching Nicodemus, and John offers us hope that if we provide the welcoming atmosphere, they will come with their late-night questions. Not in classes, not even in small groups, but in quiet intimacy with a respected mentor, evangelization of our young adults can and does happen.

The particular genius of John's brand of storytelling seems designed for this group of young adults. This is the information generation. Throughout their lives they have been bombarded with facts and statistics. The multiple stories of the synoptics with parable after parable, miracle after miracle, are similar to the culture that has overwhelmed them. They hunger for one story, told in depth, that contains the whole message. They hunger for one miracle that embodies the whole of healing, an individualized tale for an individualized generation. This principle lies at the heart of the structure of the fourth Gospel.

Just as Nicodemus models their intellectual seeking, the woman at the well embodies their struggle with relationships (John 4:1–42). They are the children of divorce, the ones afraid to make a permanent commitment because the permanent commitments that shaped their own lives did not last. Jesus invites them to find life in him.

The young boy who appears only in John's description of the feeding of the multitude cries out to their need to believe that the little they have to offer can make a difference in the face of so much hunger. John, more than any of the synoptics, gives us the friends of Jesus, the relationships to which this generation has assigned the importance that ours once gave to marriage. From the beloved disciple himself, to his last miracle performed for his friend Lazarus, John stresses relationships of equality and friendship.

For John, the Last Supper has no rite of breaking the bread and sharing the cup; the Eucharist in John is a rite of service. "If I, your Lord and Teacher, have washed your feet, you also ought to wash one another's feet" (John 13:14). These are profoundly important words for a generation short on symbol and ritual and long on service.

Jesus' dying words in John are not about redemption and forgiveness; he is busy taking care of his mother. Just as his public life began with concern for his mother, it ends in concern for his mother. Even the Resurrection narratives in John take on the quality of personal commitment, "Simon son of John, do you love me?" (John 21:15) is the question Jesus asks at a quiet breakfast by the shore, in contrast to the commission in the synoptics to "Go therefore and make disciples of all nations" (Matt. 28:19).

If we could begin to understand this generation as a different gospel, perhaps we would be willing to accept that their differing perception of the truth may still be true. Perhaps accepting this truth would free us to listen to the word of God as it is proclaimed in their lives, not to bring them "back," but to help us move forward together. When we are able to listen more openly and honestly to this generation, I suspect they will be ready to ritualize with us.

In John's Gospel, Jesus promises Peter that if he loves, he will eventually be led where he does not choose to go. Are we willing to take that risk?

OLD IN NEVER NEVER LAND

Wendy had decided to leave Never Never Land,
that place where you never grow old
and every tree is grown for climbing on
and every brook beckons bare toes;
where there is always the villain
with his ticking clocks
and his plans of deceit;
where there is always a hero
a heroine
an adventure

The adventures had grown stale,
and each new one, similar to the one before.
No one ever really won
or lost

That place where you never grow old . . .

When she looked at her reflection
the face of a child looked back.
But inside, she felt like an ancient
one who had experienced the world
and sucked from it all its vitality and excitement,
one whose sole contentment was found
in a rocking chair,
a painting,
a memory.

There had to be more
it was time

So she returned to her mother's world
where humanity races life
and trees are made into houses
and bridges are built over brooks;
where there is sometimes no villain
but more often, no hero
there is always an adventure, though
and there is true victory
and defeat . . .
That place where people do, indeed, grow old

In this new place
people are constantly changing
doing new things
thinking new thoughts
here, with every answered question
a million more are born

It was strange
in a world of perpetual youth
she had felt old,
in this world permeated with antiquity
where the rings on the tree trunks multiply
and the brooks know countless generations of bare
        feet
Wendy was young.

—LIZ, AGE EIGHTEEN

CONCLUSION

ADOLESCENCE is over. Few recognize this as clearly and poignantly as Liz did at eighteen, but all our young adults are aware that the familiar sidewalks Jon spoke of in the beginning of this book have run out. But "who really knows what they want to do at eighteen?" Steve's question lingers in the air.

Today it is not a simple step from adolescence to adulthood. Our young adults' search for identity has been complicated by prolonged education, the escalating complexity of the job market, and the insecurity that has been part of the world and the relationships that have shaped them. Adolescence finished, they linger in the vestibule of adulthood in a new stage of development we have called postadolescence.

There are no familiar landmarks, no Dr. Spock to tell us what to expect next, no lengthy psychological studies to assure us of what is "normal." I am reminded of something the theologian Thomas Merton once said when asked to show the pathway to prayer. He said it was like asking for the path through a snow-covered field. You simply walk across the field and then there will be a path.

Part of our struggle today is arriving at that simple realization. We are not pathfinders. We are path makers. We are setting the pace, naming the landmarks, and creating the myths that future Spocks will document for later generations. It has been the hope of this book to begin that conversation.

Many of our postadolescents have returned to "home base." Years of childhood games have taught them it is the place where you can stop to catch your breath, the place where you can never be tagged out. One young woman in her twenties, reflecting on the label of her generation called "X," suggested it was the "X" in "Pedestrian Xing." They are people journeying from one side to the other who need others to watch out for them as they make their way across. I suspect it is a description not so much of a generation, but of this particular stage of postadolescence. And we parents welcome them, or at least accept them, as we struggle to understand a journey we did not make.

Yet we see our fingerprints all over the people they have become. Our own self-images have grown entangled in their identity, even as they struggle to know who they are. They work at forgiving us for the ways we have failed them as parents, while we parents are faced with a far more daunting task of not only forgiving *them* their mistakes, but of forgiving *ourselves* their mistakes.

We are learning to let them go before they have actually "left," and they are striving to become emotionally independent while they are still financially dependent. In the process we are developing a new, *interdependent* family life. Or perhaps we are simply rediscovering an older way of being family that flourished before independence became the ultimate goal of maturity.

Though many of our young adults have left our churches, they have not turned away from God. Their individualized spirituality challenges us in those spots where we have grown too comfortable. Their spiritual journey through postadolescence has led many of us parents to a more conscious examining and a more wholehearted reclaiming of our own faith, a reclaiming that often includes the very rituals and community they question.

Some are reaching the end of this postadolescent stage having achieved a strong, adult friendship with their parents that our generation took many more years to establish. The extended time of interdependence has frequently given them an appreciation of family and a sense of the generations and traditions that many of us did not experience until we had children of our own. Our middle child, Becky, expressed that for us most clearly.

She was preparing for her wedding and setting up her new home when she approached me with her problem.

"I can't find the blessing for the door. I've looked everywhere. How can I have a home without a door blessing?"

I had no idea what she meant. She was astonished by my puzzlement and whirled me around to face our own front door. Next to it hung a framed "Old Irish Blessing." I realized it had hung there all the years of her life. Its primary significance to her Dad and me was that it had been a wedding present embroidered by a well-loved student. It had always been by the door simply because it seemed like the appropriate place to hang something that began, "May the road rise up to meet you."

Becky explained:

It's just always been there, and I guess that's why I thought of it as the door blessing. It's the line that begins "until we meet again . . ." that I heard as a blessing for all our comings and goings. It is a symbol to me of my family of origin, a sign that our home was a place where everyone was always welcome.

I'm not a child anymore. It's now my responsibility. I want to create a home that will be as open and as welcoming as the home that you and Dad gave us.

And so to all who are beginning the journey into adulthood, who are leaving "Never Never Land" for the "land of your mother's" and who take so much of us with you:

> May the road rise up to meet you,
> May the wind be always at your back,
> May the sun shine warm upon your face,
> And the rains fall soft upon your fields,
> And until we meet again
> May God hold you in the palm of his hand.[1]

BIBLIOGRAPHY

BOOKS

Arnold, Johann Christoph. *Endangered: Your Child in a Hostile World.* Farmington, PA: Plough Publishing Co., 2000.

Carter, B., and M. McGoldrick, eds. *The Changing Family Life Cycle: A Framework for Family Therapy.* 2nd ed. Boston, MA: Allyn and Bacon, 1989.

Durkheim, Emile. Translated by George Simpson. *The Division of Labor in Society.* New York: Free Press of Glencoe, 1964.

Gross, Edith Henkin. *And You Thought It Was All Over.* New York: St. Martin's Press, 1985.

Haley, J. *Leaving Home.* New York: McGraw-Hill, 1980.

Kunstler, James Howard. *Geography of Nowhere.* New York: Simon and Schuster, 1993.

Putnam, Robert. *Bowling Alone: The Collapse and Revival of the American Community.* New York: Simon and Schuster, 2000.

Wallulis, Jerald. *The New Insecurity: The End of the Standard Job and Family.* Albany, NY: State University of New York Press, 1998.

ARTICLES

Bernard, Joan Kelly. "Bringing up the Twenty-Somethings." *Newsday,* 5 February 1994.

Carey, Benedict, Katherine Riffin, and John Hastings. "Adult Children Fare Well at Home." *Health Magazine,* October 1994.

Clemens, Audra W., and Leland J. Axelson. "The Not-so-empty Nest: The Return of the Fledgling Adult." *Family Relations* 34, 1985.

Hartung, Beth, and Kim Sweeney. "Why Adult Children Return Home." *Social Science Journal,* October 1991.

Hochschild, Arlie Russell. "Coming of Age, Seeking an Identity." *The New York Times,* 8 March 2000.

Johnson, Patrick, and William K. Wilkinson. "The 'Re-Nesting' Effect: Implications for Family Development." *Family Journal,* April 1995.

ENDNOTES

CHAPTER 1
1. U.S. Census Bureau, 1996. Sixty-seven percent of high school graduates attend college.

2. Term coined by Carter and McGoldrick, *The Changing Family Life Cycle: A Framework for Family Therapy,* 2nd ed. (Boston, MA: Allyn and Bacon, 1989).

3. Joan Kelly Bernard. "Bringing Up the Twenty-Somethings," *Newsday,* 5 February 1994.

4. Edith Henkin Gross uses the term *postadolescent rapprochement* to describe this time of reintegration. *And You Thought It Was All Over* (New York: St. Martin's Press, 1985).

CHAPTER 2
1. Emile Durkheim, translated by George Simpson, *The Division of Labor in Society* (New York: Free Press of Glencoe, 1964).

2. Kim Clark, "Why It Pays to Quit," *U.S. News and World Report,* 1 November 1999.

3. Arlie Russell Hochschild, "Coming of Age, Seeking an Identity," *The New York Times,* 8 March 2000.

4. "My Way," words by Paul Anka, popularized by Frank Sinatra, 1967.

CHAPTER 3
1. Robert Frost, "The Death of the Hired Man," in *North of Boston,* 2nd ed. (New York: Henry Holt and Co., 1915).

2. U.S. Census Bureau, 1996.

3. Beth Hartung and Kim Sweeney, "Why Adult Children Return Home," *Social Science Journal,* October 1991.

4. *Ibid.*

5. Computers, in less than one generation, have gone from luxury, to convenience, to absolute necessity for some jobs and educational programs. Running hot water, a luxury in my youth of boiling water for weekly baths, is a necessity in a society where people are expected to shower and shampoo daily.

6. See chapter 2, "A Sense of Self."

7. James Howard Kunstler, *Geography of Nowhere* (New York: Simon and Schuster, 1993).

8. "Mira," *Carnival* (musical), music and words by Bob Merrill, 1961.

CHAPTER 4
1. Rainer Maria Rilke, as quoted by Martha Hickman in the epigraph to *Such Good People* (New York: Warner Books, 1996).

2. Patrick Johnson and William K. Wilkerson, "The 'Re-Nesting' Effect: Implications for Family Development," *Family Journal,* April 1995.

3. *Ibid.*

4. *Ibid.*

CHAPTER 5
1. Elizabeth E. Chesto, *A Finger-Painted World* (Hales Corner, WI: Sheed and Ward, 1998).

2. Johann Christoph Arnold, *Endangered: The Heart of Your Child* (Farmington, PA: Plough Publishing Co., 2000).

3. Arlie Russell Hochschild, "Coming of Age, Seeking an Identity," *The New York Times,* 8 March 2000.

4. *Statistical Abstracts of the United States,* U.S. Census Bureau, 1999.

5. Jerald Wallulis, *The New Insecurity: The End of the Standard Job and Family* (Albany, NY: State University of New York Press, 1998).

6. Robert D. Putnam, *Bowling Alone* (New York: Simon and Schuster, 2000).

7. *Webster's Collegiate Dictionary* (New York: Random House, 1990).

CHAPTER 6
1. William Damon, *The Moral Child: Nurturing Children's Natural Moral Growth* (New York: The Free Press, 1988).

CHAPTER 7
1. A Gallup poll conducted in December 1999 found that 83 percent of young adults believe in God, and 11 percent believe in the concept of a universal spirit or higher power. An August 2000 poll reveals that only 36 percent of these young adults are attending religious services.

2. Michael Crosby, OFM, *Spirituality of the Beatitudes: Matthew's Challenge for First World Christians* (Maryknoll, NY: Orbis, 1981).

CONCLUSION
1. An old Irish blessing, Anonymous.